Vicky's I

John Prater

CAMBRIDGE
UNIVERSITY PRESS

Vicky found a box. It was upside-down.
She turned it over.

A voice said, "Thank you." It was a pirate.
He was holding an old map with a cross on it.

"Hello, Vicky," said the pirate. "Climb aboard. This map shows me where to find my buried treasure."

"Hurray!" said Vicky. "Let's go!" The box
took off. Vicky put on her pirate hat.

"Where's your treasure buried?" asked Vicky.
"On a warm, sunny island," said the pirate.
It began to snow. "Are we going the right
way?" asked Vicky.

The pirate's nose turned blue. He looked
at his map. "I'm sure this is the right way,"
he said.

"We should be flying over mountains soon," said the pirate. "Can you see them?"

Then he saw land far away. "Over there!" shouted the pirate. "Look at those snowy mountains. We *are* going the right way."

"But those aren't mountains," said Vicky.
"Those are tall buildings. We're lost."

"No, no," said the pirate, pointing to the map. "Look. We're here. We have to cross a sandy desert next."

"But this isn't a desert," said Vicky, "it's
a jungle. We're still lost."
The pirate scratched his head.

Vicky said, "Let me look at the map."
Then she said, "You silly pirate. You've got it
the wrong way up!"

Now, at last, they knew where to go.
They soon found the treasure island.

The box landed near the cross, and then they began to dig. They soon found the treasure chest.

But the chest was empty.
The pirate sat down and began to cry.
"Boo, hoo! My treasure's gone."

"Don't cry," said Vicky. "Wipe your eyes."
So the pirate took out his handkerchief.
There was all his treasure!

The pirate jumped for joy. The treasure
had been in his pocket all the time!

Vicky wanted to go home.
The pirate was still being silly when the box flew into the air.

The pirate looked at the map. "We should soon be flying over the Great Blue Lake," he said.

But the pirate was wrong.
"Not again!" said Vicky.

"And now," said the pirate, "we should be near the dark forest." Just then, the box landed in Vicky's garden.

Vicky turned the map round. She thanked
the pirate and said goodbye.

Dad came out. "Can you show me where your new friend lives?" he said. "I can't find it on this map."